In Times Like These

Dr. Bernice N. King-Strong

authorHOUSE®

AuthorHouse™
1663 Liberty Drive
Bloomington, IN 47403
www.authorhouse.com
Phone: 833-262-8899

Published by AuthorHouse   03/15/2023

ISBN: 979-8-8230-0344-5 (sc)
ISBN: 979-8-8230-0343-8 (e)

Library of Congress Control Number: 2023904653

Print information available on the last page.

Any people depicted in stock imagery provided by Getty Images are models, and such images are being used for illustrative purposes only. Certain stock imagery © Getty Images.

Unless otherwise indicated, Scripture quotations are taken from the King James Version (KJV)- public domain.

This book is printed on acid-free paper.

For

My Children

The late Brandon LeNorman Strong
Even though you are gone, I still gain inspiration from your spirit.

Carmen Bernice Strong Echols
Your tenacity and ever driving force propels me to strive
beyond the limits of whatever could hold me back.

Adrienne Bernice Strong
Your quiet manner, strength, and sound reasoning helped
to center my thoughts when I wandered off.

Epigraph

In Times Like These

We must learn the lessons of studying HIS word and work, and by confessing our sin. The Lord is faithful to forgive us. Our spirituality helps us to allow the Holy Spirit we trust to direct our path. If you feel there is some force that you are lacking that would cause you to enjoy life more fully, pray for guidance from the Holy Spirit. It will help you to find peace and set you on a path to take control of your destiny.

Acknowledgements

My deepest appreciation to my friend, Rev. Dr. Willa Ross for contributing two chapters to this book, and for her gracious reading of the first draft. Thanks to Dr. LeNorman Strong for writing the foreword to this book. I wish to thank Dr. Walter Gibson Jr. for his encouragement to get my manuscript off the desk and into a publisher's hands.

Foreword

In her book, *In Times Like These,* Dr. Bernice King-Strong provides readers with a biblical study resource that serves as a guide for dealing with life's challenges in times like the ones we are currently living through. She is led by her spiritual insights and life-long commitment to our Lord and Savior Jesus Christ. Dr. King-Strong calls upon her more than 35 years of educational leadership, her experiences as a certified counselor, and her experiences as a mother and wife, to share this spirit-led book that guides readers through life experiences that sometimes challenge our spirituality. You can sense her encounters as a Christian educator and missionary by way of the themes she weaves throughout the book. She pairs life encounters with biblical references that help the reader to connect their situation with the Word from the Lord in a way that soothes the soul and frees the spirit to sour in thankfulness for the Lord's blessings.

Every chapter of the book provides readers with a specific topic of focus, often with helpful information about the topic. She provides a scripture and questions for reflection that help the reader to connect the topic with the Word. She closes each chapter with a reflection sheet for reader notes, and a prayer. I plan to utilize this book in my daily devotion to help me connect with the spiritual side of my being and to bring more peace into my life.

I hope that you will be as blessed as I have been in my journey through this wonderful gift from one of God's servants.

Introduction

Have you ever sat and pondered how our world became so messed up? Have you imagined ways in which it could be better, and contemplated what you might do to be part of the solution to problems? Everyone wants happiness and fulfilment in their lives. Living a happy life is possible. What it takes is a reset of our mindset. First, we must acknowledge that God wishes for his children to enjoy life and enjoy it more abundantly. This is his promise to us; we must embrace it. How do we do that? Secondly, we must tap into the source that helps and comforts us along this journey. This source is the Holy Spirit. The power of the Holy Spirit is ever present with us, quietly waiting for us to acknowledge its presence. Thirdly, we must rely on our faith and believe that all things are possible and that there is nothing too hard for God to handle.

Everyone has moments when they feel as though life has kicked them in the teeth or has sucker punched them in the gut. Trust me, I have been in that state of mind too. You may ask, how did I overcome the distress, fatigue, and yes the doubt that I felt at times? Understand that it takes a willingness and determination on our parts to live a life where we are constantly striving to make things better for ourselves and those we love.

How do you summon the strength to go on in difficult times? You realize that seasons come and go. One day we may be on cloud nine, the next we are full of the blues. Our trials help to build our fortitude. We often emerge from tragedy and heartache stronger than we were before. We only need to look around us and see the beauty that has been created by God for the enjoyment of womankind and mankind. We can calm our spirits and have peace in our souls knowing that the Lord cares for the birds of the air and plants on the earth, and that we are his most cherished creation; He only wants the best for his children.

When Christ left us on earth after he ascended to be with the Father, he did not leave us alone, but left us a comforter. This comforter is the Holy Spirit, the third person of the *Holy Trinity*. *The Holy Spirit* was not created by the Father or the Son but has always existed with them and is eternal (Hebrews 9:14).

Part 1: A look at spirituality and how we fit into the milieu of thought in America. We will unpack what it means to be religious and spiritual, spiritual and not religious, thus identifying as none of the above:

Overview

Although there are many religious beliefs throughout the world and the Western world specifically, we will concentrate on Christianity in America. For example, we will speak about

1. Where the Holy Spirit comes from
2. Individual spirituality vs religions in American lives
3. How far we have come from the founding fathers belief in one centering religious belief for a country

Part 2: Allowing God to speak to us and having appreciation for the mindfulness of God as he has created us in his image.

For example:

1. Bible characters encounter with God
2. Being present so that God can speak to us
3. The uniqueness of a man or woman
4. Finding value in one's own uniqueness

Part 3: There will be people who will present false doctrines to the multitudes. How do we discern what is the truth from God and turn away from false prophets?

1. Stop worrying about what is happening in your life.
2. Embracing a victorious attitude

3. Encountering wolves that are disguised to make you think they are true believers in Christ
4. No fretting allowed

Part 4: We can rest assured that God has our back although we do not always feel his presence. Know that he is always with us. He is omnipotent, and omnipresent now and forever.

1. Finding refuge and solace in him
2. Be courageous even when you do not feel like it.
3. Resolve to renew one's faith in God
4. Realize that we live in a "*feel-good*" world. That is not the life that God promised us. There will be thistles and thorns that we each will encounter.

Prologue

This book is written for an intended audience of young adults and senior readers to use as a guide to contemplate and reflect upon challenges of life—small and large. It can be used as a resource for those participating in Christian organizations, Bible study, or small circle groups affiliated with larger parent organizations. It is written from a Christian perspective; the landscape referred to is the United States of America.

All references to Spirituality refer to this author's understanding of the Gospel of Jesus Christ and have nothing to do with the underworld, fortune telling, ghosts, any practices of witchcraft, or things paranormal. Spirituality is defined by this author as having constant communication with the Trinity—God the Father, Jesus Christ the Son, and the Holy Spirit. The word Spirituality will be used when referring to the term Holy Spirit.

We deal with many challenges as well as joys in our lives. As we travel along life's journey each of us can experience these occasions in a unique way. We learn strategies to cope that can assist in understanding what is important in our lives. The outcomes of our challenges and joys are often predicated on our inner strength, outward resources, and mindset. Our spirituality is a very necessary part of our existence. Possibly one of the most neglected members of Trinity is the Holy Spirit. Relying on the Holy spirit is critical to our spiritual growth and salvation. It helps us to make meaning out of a world that is constantly evolving; at times chaotically and helps us to understand what happens to us and the why, and how of it.

The Holy Spirit has always been with us since the formation of the world. It is a gift to all children of God, and we do not have to earn it. The Holy Spirit's purpose is to guide us through lessons that teach us to be obedient, courageous, give understanding, and helps us to enjoy the full benefits of the life God intended for his children. Not all people are religious or believe in God the creator but may have a central force to which they subscribe to make sense of this planet on which we live.

There is so much about life that is yet to be understood. However, we learn to cope with life as we move along in time. The ever-changing world in which we live throws us curve balls every now and then. These curve balls cause us to have a plethora of emotions. It is okay to feel afraid and sad at times, but there is no need to, nor should one stay in a state of despair. Spiritual support of others and our own spirituality can help us through trying experiences. It takes belief, effort, and faith, to grow into a life that is full of joy. We have the inner fortitude to speak into existence living a joyous life *In Times Like These.*

As the hard work is done to avoid becoming burdened or victimized by the many negative forces around us, we must remind ourselves about our spirituality. We must live out God's purpose for our lives.

At the conclusion of studying this book, Christians and others who identify as non-believers can come to know Jesus Christ and develop an understanding and a deeper relationship with him. It is my hope that readers discover and rediscover the degree to which all can use the faith and spirituality that presently abide within us to conquer obstacles that are encountered daily.

Questions to Consider

What do you hope to gain by reading/studying this book?

_____

_____

_____

_____

Prayer

Dear Lord, open our eyes in order that we might see.
Grant us knowledge and wisdom to be the best that we can be.
Help us to rely on you for everything.
For you are our all in all. Amen

— 1 —

Our Beginning

We enter this world small, naked, and cold. We leave the warmth and comfort of our mothers which we have known for months. At birth we are then thrust into a foreign world full of people we do not know, surroundings that are unfamiliar, and are forced to breathe cold air into our lungs under bright lights. Our first encounter is to be slapped by some unfamiliar human and then tossed about to this one and that one before being given back to the one with whom we are most familiar. After spending only seconds with our mother, we are whisked off to a steel scale and then into a nursery where we are placed in a hard plastic bed.

Our entry into this world is violent. It gives us an indication of what this world has to offer. At our earliest existence we come to know that all is not warm and cozy. Our birth is an indication that there will be more roughness to come. In this life there will be heartaches, bumps and suffering as long as we live.

When we return to God, some of the same rituals will repeat themselves. We will be taken from the physical world where we once lived and worked, put on a steel slab just like the weighing scale, taken from our families, put in a box, and be with unfamiliar people in the morgue, and dirt will be thrown in our faces.

The Good news is, at the moment of death, we will have the familiar feeling of warmth and security we felt while being protected by our mother. For you see, we have a heavenly father that takes us back unto himself at the moment of death; and we can stay with him forever and exist under his protection if we have believed and followed the life he has set before us.

Just like our earthly parents cared for us and protected us until we could care for ourselves, Jesus has left us a comforter that counsels and comforts us all the days of our lives no matter the age, until we return to the Father. That comforter's name is none other than the *Holy Spirit*. I invite you to get to know him. You just might be surprised about how connecting into the Holy Spirit will enrich your life and how your mindset will change to allow you to trust when you are facing difficult times.

God does not leave us helpless to fight the battle alone in a world of sin. He knows that people will sin since the sins of Adam and Eve in the garden of Eden. Sin has been a phenomenon for all Christian people. There had to be a way for man to be reconciled to God. Therefore, he sent his son Jesus to die on the cross to bear our sin and through him, man could be forgiven for the sins that God knew would be committed. This forgiveness does not mean for us to continue to sin over and over because we know that we will be forgiven. We are to repent of our sins and intend to lead a new life free from past sins.

Questions for Consideration:

If the Holy Spirit is our comforter, why do we feel so bad when things happen to good people?

_____.

_____.

Why is there so much turmoil in the world? Wars, famine?

_____?

_____?

Do you feel comforted by the Holy Spirit when you hear of human trafficking, child molestation, pestilence and disease? What about so many are dying from senseless killing of the innocent? Do you feel comforted when gender and/or racial discrimination is perpetrated against you and /

or against our brothers and sisters? Explain your answers for each of these question below.

_____

_____

_____

_____

_____

_____

_____.

— 2 —

Are we Losing our
Spiritual Intelligence?

A re we losing our spirituality as human beings? Not to equate church affiliation with spirituality, more people in America are becoming unchurched, and they are okay with no church affiliation or religious affiliation. There has been a decline in religious affiliation and belief in God, in America. The American Christian majority has been in decline for many years. A study done by the PEW Research Center shows that as of 2020, only sixty-four percent of people living in America who identify as Americans say they are Christian. In 1970, that number was ninety percent. According to the PEW Research Center 2015. America is becoming less religious. A survey conducted of 35,000 American adults finds that the percentage who say they believe God, pray daily and regularly go to church or other religious services all have declined to a modest degree.

In recent years, the Pew Research Center study also shows a great deal of stability in America. The recent decrease in religious beliefs and behaviors is largely due to the people who identify as "none". According to PEW (2015) there is a growing minority of Americans, particularly in the Millennial generation, who say they do not belong to any organized faith. However, among the roughly three-quarters of American adults who do claim a religion, there has been no apparent drop in most measures of religious commitment. By some traditional measures, religiously affiliated Americans are, on average, even more devout than they were a few years ago (PEW, 2015).

The Religious Landscape Study (RLS) of 2014 is a follow-up survey on religion in America, originally conducted in 2007. An initial report on the findings from the 2014 study released in May 2015, described the changing size and demographic characteristics of the nation's major religious groups. This report focuses on Americans' religious beliefs and practices and assess how they have changed in recent years.

The portion of American adults who say they believe in God, while still remarkably high by comparison with other advanced industrial countries, has declined modestly from 92% to 89% since PEW Research Center conducted its first Landscape Study in 2007. The portion of Americans who say they are sure that God exist dropped from 71% in 2007 to 63% in 2014. The percentage who say they pray every day, attend religious services regularly and consider religion to be very important in their lives also have been indicated downward by small but statistically significant margins (PEW, 2015).

The decrease in traditional religious beliefs and practices coincides with changes in the religious composition of the American public. A growing number of Americans are religiously unaffiliated, including some who self-identify as atheist or agnostic as well as many who describe their religion as nothing. Altogether, the "none" now accounts for 23% of the adult population, increasing from 16% in 2007.

Research indicates that many Americans say they are spiritual but not religious. Statistics from the PEW research study says that 48% say they are both religious and spiritual, while 6% say they are religious but not spiritual. Another 18% answer both questions negatively, saying they are neither religious nor spiritual. A total of 54% of American adults think of themselves as religious- a decrease in 11 points since 2012- while far more (75%) say they are spiritual, a figure that has remained relatively steady in recent years (PEW Research Center, 2017).

Many who are in the "spiritual but not religious" category seldom have religious observances or attend religious services. Those who identify as "spiritual but not religious" are equal between men and women. Sixty-two percent of the American men account for those who say they are neither religious nor spiritual (PEW Research Center, 2017).

Questions for Consideration

What does it mean to be spiritual but not religious?

_____

_____

_____

_____

_____

_____

_____

_____

Summary

Although the Holy Spirit has always existed, a person cannot feel the Holy Spirit on their own. You must be open to letting the spirit be activated in you. God does not force anything upon us. We must invite him in and He will be willing to come into our hearts and dwell with us forever. We must open ourselves in a position to accept the means of grace. For it is grace that is given by God. We have the choice to cooperate with it or not. Grace is a gift from God. A gift we take for granted and do not deserve.

The Holy Spirit works within us to make us holy. The Holy Spirit is the indwelling within us. The indwelling is recognizable in believers by the striving for a perfection that we display as we try to live a life pleasing to God. The Holy Spirit aligns us with the original intent of God for his creation.

Prayer

Holy Father, help us to understand what your Holy
Spirit does in the life of a Christian.
Help us to know that the Holy Spirit is our comforter and helper.
Help us to know that the spirit gives us our power.
Allow the spirit to fill us up. Amen

— 3 —

Covid-19 Did a Number on US

You shall serve the LORD your God, and he
will bless your bread and your water, and I will
take sickness away from among you.
Exodus 23:25

As a nation, we have been shaken to our very core by the impact of the Covid-19 Pandemic. The distress economic, educational, psychological, physical, and spiritual created because of the global pandemic and its variants is evident all around us. With so many people succumbing to the virus at alarming rates, the lives of many Americans were turned upside down and inside out. None of us felt safe anymore. Everywhere we turned there was chaos. The grocery store shelves were constantly being emptied. Personal protective supplies such as Lysol, toilet paper, masks and paper towels were in high demand and in short supply. Prices increased on almost everything we needed to purchase. Tempers flared in every corner, and we became suspicious of each other as though we were aliens. How quickly we turned on each other.

Some scholars wrote about the virus and compared it to Biblical plagues that occurred in the books of Exodus and Revelation (Clay, 2020). Some declared that Covid-19 was God's judgment on an unrighteous people. Although the plagues in Exodus 7: 14-12:36 were plagues of blood, frogs, gnats, flies, livestock, boils, hail, locusts, and the death of the firstborn, the sting of Covid felt like all of these wrapped in one. Likewise, the plagues spoken about in Revelation 11:6 and Revelation 15:1 (KJV) report water turning to blood and seeing the wrath of God; we are not in Egypt, but felt like we were suffering the wrath of God in an unprecedented way not witnessed in decades. The World Health Organization (WHO) reported that more than 500,000 deaths had occurred at the time of this writing, and the number of fatalities attributed to the virus continues to climb.

Christians, as well as other religious groups wondered if the end was near. We wondered how a God that loved us so much could allow so much pain to consume so many in such a brief period. It was like fighting a war against an invisible enemy. We can see soldiers shooting and fighting each other in war movies on our television screens or at the movies, but this was an enemy that we could not reach out and touch. We felt abandoned. Even many Christians lost hope and felt that our faith just was not enough to get us through the challenging times.

To add injury to insult, our houses of worship had to be closed for health and safety reasons; relegating congregants to social media to engage in collective worship services. Some people had no such devices or did not know how to gain access to services even if they had the equipment. The world was and is in a state of confusion. One of the most devastating results of the pandemic was the inability to have a funeral when someone died, or a delay of the ceremony because there were so many dead people scheduled for services ahead of your loved one. Personally, I thought, this must be what hell feels like albeit we were experiencing it on earth. Covid-19 is still with us, but just like everything else we have grown accustomed to adapting our own safe practices--masking up, getting vaccinated and staying away from large gatherings.

Some might say that the lack of contact with loved ones during hospitalization for the severely ill sped up their demise and led to their death. The lack of spiritual care that patients could have otherwise received from clergy, family, because of necessary restrictions on visitations, had they been allowed, may have prolonged their life or given them the will to live. Conversely, the lack of spiritual care is believed by many to have been a cause for their lack of progress and hastened their demise (Hall, 2020).

The PEW Research Study (2017) states that fewer Americans identify as having religious affiliation or spiritual belief in a supreme being. Meanwhile, religious, or non-religious, the ministry of presence helps any human to make sense of what is going on in a world that was turned upside down literally overnight.

Christians and non-Christians alike experienced a myriad of emotions. We displayed emotions of anger, depression, disillusionment, grief, helplessness, and sadness; all troubling from a mental health perspective. We tried desperately to hold on to our spiritual grounding. *In Times Like These*, it was necessary to force ourselves to see the good in what someone did. It was as though we were looking for a single rose to grow out of the concrete, forcing its way through four feet of snow. The way many survived the horrific initial devastation of the pandemic was by reminding themselves and others that even though we were experiencing despair, it would not be this way always. It was a way of not allowing the devastation to consume us. Yes, COVID-19 did a number on us. But God! Here we are still standing, and we are still here. Praise be to God. Perhaps that is a message He was sending us.

I cannot answer why so many died. I do not have an answer as to why our loved one(s) had to be in that number. Only God knows. Many things that have happened and will continue to happen will never make sense to us. The Bible teaches us that everything works out for our good. Hopefully, one day we will be able to reconcile what happened to us all during the pandemic. But, for now, know that it is in God's hands and His hands are big enough to hold all of us.

Questions for Consideration

Were you or someone you know on the verge of giving up during the pandemic?

_____

_____

_____

_____

_____

_____

_____

_____

Who or what kept you spiritually grounded?

_____

_____

_____

_____

_____

_____

_____

_____

_____

_____

How will you cope differently if another pandemic of such magnitude happens soon?

_____

_____

_____

_____

_____

_____

_____

_____

_____

_____

Summary

No matter what happens in life, be it a plague, virus; or other calamity that befalls us, we must trust God and seek his guidance. There comes a time in all our lives that we choose to trust God or be bitter in our hearts because of circumstances beyond our control. Anger and bitterness toward God serves no good purpose. For Christians, anger and bitterness can cause us to reject God. We must guard against losing the promise of God, which is eternal life, because of our own actions and emotions. We must love God with all our being, heart, and mind.

Amid the chaos and grief, we experienced, during the pandemic and life in general, God is still on the throne. Let us not forget the sovereignty of God. Nothing that happens is a surprise to him. He knew the virus would come. God is worthy of our confidence in His authority and sovereignty. He is omnipotent and omnipresent. God sees and hears us when we call upon Him and He will be merciful unto us and bless us.

Prayer

Lord hold us in the palm of your hand.
Keep us from hurt and danger.
Keep your hedge of protection around us.
Bless us whenever we go out and when we come in.
We will be careful to give you honor and glory. Amen

— 4 —

For Everything There is
a Time and a Season

*A time for every purpose under heaven: a time
to be born and a time to die; a time to plant,
and a time to pluck what is planted.*
Ecclesiastes 3: 1-

In Christian theology, the Holy Spirit is believed to perform specific divine functions in the life of the individual Christian and/or the Church. The action of the Holy Spirit is seen as an essential part of the bringing of the person to the Christian faith. The Holy Spirit is God, the Third person of the Trinity, coequal with the Father and the Son, Jesus Christ. The Holy Spirit was not created by the Father or the Son but has always existed and is eternal (Hebrews 9:14).

In the Gospel of John, Jesus refers to the Holy Spirit in three ways: Holy Spirit, Spirit of Truth and Parklets (Advocate, Counselor, Helper, and Comforter). The Holy Spirit has specific roles that it performs in the life of the Christian. According to Noyes (2022), the roles of the Holy Spirit:

(1) The Holy Spirit teaches us and reminds us.
    The Holy Spirit is a helper to us and serves as an advocate for us.
(2) The Holy Spirit provides wise counsel.

The Holy Spirit will prove the sin, righteousness, and judgment of the world.

(3) Dwells in us.

The Holy Spirit is God's presence in the lives of believers.

(4) The Holy Spirit is where revelation, wisdom, and power originate from. God gives His followers the Holy Spirit so we may know Him better. Christians have access to power, revelation, and wisdom from the *Holy Spirit* when it comes on you, and you will be my witnesses in Jerusalem, and in all Judea and Samaria, and to the ends of the earth.

(5) Guides to All Truth and Knowledge of What is to Come

The Holy Spirit tells what is yet to come. The Holy Spirit is called the "Spirit of Truth."

(6) Gives gifts of the spirit to Believers

These gifts are wisdom, knowledge, and power. These gifts are not to be coveted or boasted about but used for the benefit of others.

(7) Saved if you believe in your heart that Christ died and was raised from the dead.

When you believed, you were saved until the day of redemption. We are granted eternal life through the Holy Spirit.

(8) The Holy Spirit enables us to bear good fruit.

The work of the Holy Spirit in a Christian's life is an ongoing process of becoming holy through sanctification.

You might ask where does the Holy Spirit come from? As mentioned earlier, the Holy Spirit is the third person in the Trinity. Jesus promised the apostles that he would send the Holy Spirit after his crucifixion and resurrection. "But the helper, the Holy Spirit, whom the Father will send in my name, he will teach you all things" (John 14: 26 ESV).

On the day of Pentecost, the Holy Spirit descended on the Apostles and the disciples. (Acts 2), is seen as the fulfillment of the promise of an intercessor, and helper. Therefore, the Holy Spirit is a being just like the Father and Son. Our spirituality rests on the fact that the spirit lives within us and the inward and outward manifestation of the indwelling spirit is reflected in our acts of spirituality.

I remember vividly the day that I knew the Holy Spirit had descended upon me. I was a young girl of 10 years old. It was during my baptism in my home church of Texas. On that hot Sunday afternoon in August of 1965, the spirit engulfed me like a raging fire, permeating my entire being. The spirit ravaged my soul to the point of utter restlessness like a sleepless night until I came to rest at peace as a sleeping lamb cuddled beneath the warmth of a mother's cradling body. What a memorable experience that I shall never forget. I was forever changed unto a new life; one where I began to rely on the Holy Spirit to speak to me and through me. My conversion was not as a peaceful dove resting upon my shoulder as on the day of Pentecost. I was initially so set aflame that I felt I would combust at the slightest provocation. I can just imagine how some of the converts must have felt on the very day of Pentecost.

Although we are centuries past the day of Pentecost, the same Holy Spirit is with us as it was with the multitudes on that day. We are living in a season of an ever-changing world. However, the Spirit has not changed to conform to us. In this season, we must change to activate the Holy Spirit within us that is the same from the beginning. Our practices of spirituality and expressions of such change fit the times in which we live.

We are in a new season of the Christian faith. Good and dreadful things happen to us throughout life. We do not understand the meaning of it all. The world is changing in so many fields and Christianity is no different. What we once saw as a homogeneous way of practicing religion in America is no longer. The way we practice our spirituality as Christians, has evolved. For example, we have technology and use it more than ever before. We use technology to capture the practice of our spirituality by putting on full blast our rituals and methods. There is nothing wrong with technology. Except when we use our technology to totally forsake fellowship and assembly with other believers. In this season of the use of technology to conduct our worship services, we must guard against using technology only to maintain our connection to a higher power.

God, being sovereign over every aspect of our lives, does what he wants, how and when he wants to do it. What God does is right and true. We know there is nothing new under the sun. What has already happened, and what will happen in the future, have already been set in God's timing. The pandemic was no accident. God needed to get our attention and he did.

We are in a season of uncertainty. We have a new opportunity to either strengthen our relationship with the Lord or let go of an already weak connection. We continue to endure our seasons because God is there with us to sustain us through every trial and trust and believe it is for a reason.

It is said that we are in a period of the Great Apostasy, meaning that we have fallen away from the original faiths we once believed. Only one example is how some memberships have diminished in size. Christians act out behaviors that were formerly only committed by sinners, and there is less support for all things Christian. We should not be surprised. For II Thessalonians 2:1-17 reads,

"Concerning the coming of our Lord
Jesus Christ and our being gathered.
To him, we ask you, brothers, and sisters.
Do not be easily unsettled or alarmed.
By the teaching allegedly from us
Whether by prophecy or by word of
Mouth or by letter asserting that the day.
Of the Lord has already come.
Do not let anyone deceive you in any way.
For that day will not come until the rebellion
Occurs and lawlessness is revealed."

Some claim to know when the world will come to an end. No one knows when that will happen. Be aware of people predicting the end of the earth. There is no truth in their predictions. Certainly, the book of Revelation spells out for us various signs to warn of the end time. Even the angles in heaven will not know ahead of time when Christ shall descend and come back to gather up his people. Until that day comes we must endure until the end. We will need to suffer many hardships and tribulations in this life before receiving our reward.

The saying goes, "what does not kill us makes us stronger." Although, we never know the reasons God puts us through difficult and stressful seasons, as believers we hold on to the knowledge that it is for a good reason. Not all seasons are bad. As the songwriter writes, "It's your season to be blessed." (Hutchins, 2013). This song echoes the sentiment that God blesses us in due season. Our seasons belong to us and us alone. My season is not predicated on your good fortune or time of distress. God gives us all seasons at his discretion, and it is to build us up so that we may be sanctified (Mashburn, 2020).

Questions for Consideration

Is the great falling away inevitable?

_____

_____

_____

_____

_____

_____

_____

_____

How must we guard against apostasy?

_____

_____

_____

_____

_____

_____

_____

What actions should a backslider take to be in right relationship with God?

_____

_____

_____

_____

_____

_____

_____

_____

Reflect on your Holy Spirit experience: How did you know the spirit was upon you? Where were you and what were you doing?

_____

_____

_____

_____

_____

_____

_____

Describe ways in which you practice your spirituality:

_____

_____

_____

_____

_____

_____

_____

Summary:

No matter what season we find ourselves in, we must learn to be content. We need to stay prayed up because we never know what is around the next corner. However, we do not need to live as though dreadful things are the only events that will occur in our lives. There is joy as well as sadness. But life is not a rose garden. We should expect to have our share of thorns and thistles, and detours. There will be rainy as well as sunny days. Days of plenty and days of want. We must learn to look for good in whatever season we find ourselves. For surely, God keeps blessing us repeatedly.

Prayer

Lord, lead us not into temptation.
But deliver us from evil,
We accept whatever befalls us.
Knowing that you do all things well.
We rejoice in and out of season.

— 5 —

Keeping it Real

Contributed by Dr. Willa Ross

Just as I am, without one plea.
But that Thy blood was shed for me
And that Thou bid'st me come to Thee
Oh, Lamb of God, I come, I come.

One of my favorite hymns is "Just as I Am". I found it interesting that one of my favorite actresses, Cicely Tyson used it as the title of her new book, a memoir. She describes the book in this way: "Just as I am my truth, it is me, plain and unvarnished with the glitter and garland set asides". The hymn, "Just as I Am" speaks to me in many ways. However, the overriding theme for me is that God accepts me with all my flaws and scars-just as I am. I have often heard many preachers use the term, "warts and all," in their sermons. This analogy reminds me of the importance of "Keeping it Real," that I am not all that and not worthy of God's grace and mercy. Yet, God accepts me just as I am, "warts and all."

It is reassuring to know this; however, we often try desperately to cover up our warts and hide them from others. We want so much to be the person who is calm and collected. We want to be the best, top-notch, at the top of the class, the one who has all the knowledge, the one who has it going on, the one who everybody loves and respects. The problem with these impressions of ourselves is that we strive for these things, and because of our insecurities and our desire to please others, we operate out of our false selves.

In Times Like These, we must learn the lesson of *"Keeping it Real"*. Our faith in God, our spirituality is what enables us to do so. Our humanity is challenged every day. Something is always happening that needs to be fixed or taken care of. We never can relax or enjoy life. When things happen in our lives that go against who we really are in Christ, when we allow the trials in our lives to cause us to panic, when we allow the perceptions and expectations of others to direct our thoughts and our actions, we lose sight of our spirituality and the foundation of our faith. When crisis arrives in our communities or in our individual lives, and we feel as if everything is about to cave in, we must remember who we are.

Regardless of our life situations, regardless of how the winds blow in our lives, we have been chosen by God. We are a royal priesthood. We need only to remember we are made in the image of God, even in our anxiety, even when we are led by false self to do otherwise. God accepts us just as we are. No amount of pretense or deception can change this. Because we know that "trouble does not last always," and there is hope for tomorrow.

However, if we choose not to allow the Holy Spirit to infiltrate our lives, if we let others take the helm to navigate us through troubled waters, the boat will topple and sink, and we will drown in the deep waters. We lose sight of who we are and allow others, sometimes our own family and friends, to lead us in the wrong direction. When this happens, we begin to believe that God does not love us. We fail to keep it real.

Keeping it Real means, we lean not to our own understanding, but through God, we allow the Holy Spirit we trust to bring us out of the deep and direct our paths. We are intelligent, we are resilient, we are made strong in our weakness; we persevere. We acknowledge God, who is with us in all our failures, in all our brokenness for we know that God "will make a way out of no way for us."

Our dependence on the Holy Spirit helps us to "keep it real." Our spirituality gets us through the dark days. When we remember that God will never abandon us and that there is nothing that "will be able to separate us from the love of God in Christ Jesus, our Lord" (Romans 9b: NRSV), we prevail. In Times Like These we experience unspeakable joy and peace that surpasses all our understanding. **We Keep It Real.**

Questions to Consider

What thoughts or emotions lead you to depend on others more than God?

_____

_____

_____

_____

_____

_____

_____

Describe your warts.

_____

_____

_____

_____

_____

_____

_____

In what ways do you rely on God in difficult situations?

_____

_____

_____

_____

_____

_____

_____

How does your spirituality sustain you in these times?

_____

_____

_____

_____

_____

_____

_____

What Bible verse or scripture(s) help(s) you to depend on and trust in God?

_____
_____
_____
_____
_____
_____
_____

What helps you to keep it real?

_____
_____
_____
_____
_____
_____

Summary

God wants us to be authentic in all we do. No one is on top of the world all the time; it is unreasonable to think so. Keeping it real helps us to stay focused on the one true God. We care too much about what others think of us and less about how God sees us. The next time you question whether you are keeping it real or hiding behind a façade you have created, ask yourself if others can give you breath of life, add one hour to your life, give you eternal life or heal you from all diseases? If you answered no to all these questions, you have all the ingredients you need to *Keep It Real*.

Prayer

Heavenly Father, help us to abide in you.
We move and have our being through you.
Keep us from relying too much on people.
We are not perfect but grant us confidence to be enough in your sight.
Teach us to walk in the same way you walk. Amen

— 6 —

In God's Presence

Contributed by Dr. Willa Ross

Then Jacob woke from his sleep. He said,
"God is in this place-truly.
And I did not even know it.
(Genesis 28: 16- The Message Bible)

Spending time in God's presence is essential to our spirituality. We cannot know a person unless we spend time with them. How can we expect to know God if we do not spend time in God's presence? God is always with us; it is only our awareness of God's presence that impacts our spirituality. Often, we only acknowledge God's presence in worship-when we hear a good sermon, or prayer or the singing of a favorite hymn. Jesus reminds us in Matthew 28: 20 that he is with us always, even to the end of time. In Hebrews, 13:5, we read "I will never leave you or forsake you".

Our spirituality leads us to an awareness of God's continual presence in our lives. It is one thing to say, "I can feel the presence of the Lord in this place," or sing, "The presence of the Lord is here." But to know God's presence and acknowledge it is entirely different. Knowing God's presence as you sit and pray, or drive on your way to work, or sit at your desk, or cheer your favorite sports team is different. Knowing God's presence in the mundane everyday happenings of your daily life provides assurance that whatever the day brings-heartache, weariness, chaos, turmoil, sadness, depression—God's grace abounds.

To know God's grace is to sit in God's presence and to walk in God's love without fear. Richard Rohr says ". . . God does not give grace-God is grace." (Universal Christ). Being in God's presence is to truly experience God's grace and love.

One of my favorite passages of Scripture in the Old Testament is Jacob's encounter with God at Haran. After stealing his older brother, Esau's blessing from his father Isaac, Jacob finds himself in a place where he dreams of angels of God ascending and descending on a ladder. In the dream God stands beside him. God tells Jacob" ...Know that I am with you and will keep you wherever you go. For I will not leave you until I have done what I promised you. (v.15). When Jacob awakens from the dream, he says, "Surely the Lord is in this place-and I did not know it!" (v.16). Later in Chapter 32 Jacob wrestles with God and receives a blessing.

Fully knowing God's presence requires us sometimes sitting in the presence of God. Some often think that worship is the only space where God's presence can be experienced. Certainly, God is present with us in worship, however, God desires us to experience that presence more deeply. There are times when our soul thirsts for God's presence. *In Times Like These*, we need to put aside doing and just "be." To be quiet and allow God's presence to overwhelm us and bathe us in God's love. It is through Spiritual practices such as Lectio Divina and Contemplative sits, meditation and reflection, mindfulness, and other practices in which we can hear and feel God's presence in amazing and often mysterious ways. The Spirit leads us into a deeper and richer relationship with God.

We become so busy in our daily lives, going here and there—to work, school. Taking care of family, maintaining relationships, participating in civic and social events, serving on boards, and doing volunteer work, and yes church work. We take time to plan leisure and vacation time, but little time for retreats in which we could connect with God, either in small groups or individually.

Prior to the pandemic, people leading active lives had very little time to engage in consistent reflection and contemplation. This is not to say that they did not engage in times of study, meditation, and prayer. However, the pandemic presented opportunities to engage in spiritual practices and seek and experience God's presence in diverse ways and spaces.

I go back to Jacob's encounter and his non-awareness that God was present in the place with him. Only when Jacob was weary and tired of running, when he stopped doing, was he able to truly experience God's presence. He exclaimed that God's presence was formidable. As it was with Jacob, we too can get caught up in our lives, even in our responsibilities of caring for others, in our church work, and yes in practicing our spirituality, that we fail to acknowledge God's presence.

In Times Like These-civil unrest, vaccine hesitancy, spreading of disease, protests for justice and equality, partisan politics, natural disaster, white supremacy, upheaval, and threats to our democracy that we often fail to be aware of God's presence in all things going on in the world. Like Jacob, could it be that we are only aware of God's presence after we arise from our sleep? Or when we are exhausted, or weary of all the discord, or in need of God's favor. Just as God is present with us, God desires our presence as well.

"Yea, do I walk through the valley of the shadow of death,
I will not fear for God is with me."

Questions for Consideration:

What does it mean to be in God's presence?

_____

_____

_____

_____

_____

_____

_____

In what ways have you experienced God's presence?

_____

_____

_____

_____

_____

_____

_____

What spiritual practices do you engage in?

_____
_____
_____
_____
_____
_____
_____

What are your experiences?

_____
_____
_____
_____
_____
_____

Can you identify with Jacob? If so, how?

_____
_____
_____
_____
_____

Summary

Slow down. We live hurried lives. More time needs to be spent intentionally meditating on God's word. Look for moments when God's spirit is with you. Shut out the noise of the world, clear your mind, and make a practice of listening to his voice. Ask him to speak to you. Allow His spirit to engulf you and give you peace.

Prayer

Father make your presence known to us.
Remove distractions from our lives.
Hear our pleas when we call upon thee. Amen

— 7 —

Living a Spirit Filled Life

Life presents us with challenges each day of our lives. We are either coming out of a storm, going into a storm or in the present toughest trial of our life that we have ever experienced. We wonder how we will ever find peace again. We wring our hands, shed tears, and spend countless sleepless nights trying to figure out what to do. Oftentimes we may be rendered paralyzed at the thought of going on another day.

In Times Like These, we must lean not to our own understanding. Jesus Christ God's son assures us that he will be with us always. Not only must we believe in Him and trust what he says, the Bible tells us that he left His peace with us. Christ's will for us today is to trust that his purpose and motive for allowing many things to happen in our lives is to show us that all he ever wants for us is good. This belief alone is cause for us to have an abiding peace.

Trials will come on every hand. How we deal with these trials is what causes us to have peace or no peace. We must grab hold of the peace He offers and trust in him that all will be well. The greatest peace of all is realizing that one day we will be in perfect peace with our creator, Jesus hung on the cross and died so that all humankind might be reconciled to God the Father. Consequently, we can live a spirit filled life, but only by believing on Jesus Christ and that his death paid for all our transgressions. When this happens, we can all live a spirit filled life in perfect peace.

According to the Apostle Paul in the book of Ephesians 5: vs. 15-16 sets up how we can live a spirit filled life. He states, "Be careful how you walk, not as unwise men, but as wise, making the most of your time, because the days are evil (NASB). In other words, he is saying do not live a life as though there is no end. Do not be foolish in your behavior. Work while it is day and do good you can while you can. When the night comes (death) no man can work; it will be all said and done.

The world we live in would have us spend all our time worrying about the next catastrophe that may befall us. Rather than sit and anticipate some tumultuous event, we should think of a better day coming. Like in Colossians 3: 2, "set your mind on the things above." In *Times Like These,* we must be intentional and set our thoughts on being productive, such as serving God rather than evil, walking upright, keeping our minds and bodies busy with the things of God. If we are not careful, evil will keep us from living a spirit filled life. You may have heard the saying, "an idle mind is the devil's workshop." Keep your whole being actively engaged with spiritual and good things lest the devil makes room for evil and negativity to creep into our minds.

It can be easy to live a spirit-filled life if we use what we have already been given. Excerpts taken from the writings of Dr. Bill Bright entitled *"Have you made the Wonderful Discovery of the Spirit-Filled Life?"* explains in detail how living a spirit-filled life can be achieved. He first speaks of three types of people and goes in detail to explain the characteristics of each type of person. First there is the natural person. The natural person has yet to receive Christ. Therefore, being a natural man, he cannot understand the things of God. The precepts of spiritual things seem foolish to him (1 Corinthians 2:14, New American Standard Bible) NASB. Secondly, there is the Spiritual person that is directed by the Holy Spirit. The person sees Jesus' influence and direction in their life. "He who is spiritual appraises all things...we have the mind of Christ" (1 Corinthians 2: 15-16, NASB). Thirdly, the Carnal Person, one who has received Christ, but who lives in defeat because he is trying to live the Christian life in his own strength. As stated in 1Corinthians 3: 1-3, NASB "And I brethren, could not speak to you as to spiritual men, but as to men of the flesh, as to infants in Christ. I gave you milk to drink, not solid food; for you were not yet able to receive it. Indeed, even now you are not yet able, for you are still fleshly. For since there is jealously and strife among you, are not fleshly, and are you not walking like mere men?"

In contrast, (Bright) goes on to delineate what attributes the Spiritual person has. The Spiritual person has the following attributes: Christ centered, empowered by the Holy Spirit, introduces others to Christ, has an effective prayer life, understands God's word, trusts, and obeys God, experiences love, joy, peace, patience, kindness, faithfulness, gentleness, goodness, and self-control.

Christians as well as non-believers are not living life to their full potential. Bright (2022), sees the following as reasons why this is happening. First, the person is uninformed or has forgotten about God's love, forgiveness, and power (Acts 1:8) which states, "But *ye shall receive power, after that the Holy Ghost is come upon you: and ye shall be witnesses unto me both in Jerusalem and in all Judaea and in Samaria, and unto the uttermost part of the earth.*" (KJV) Second, there is an up and down spiritual experience. Third, the person does not understand themselves- he or she wants to do right but cannot. Fourth, the individual fails to draw upon the power of the Holy Spirit to live the Christian life (Galatians 5: 16-18) which states, "*This I say then, walk in the Spirit, and ye shall not fulfill the lust of the flesh. For the flesh lusted against the Spirit and the Spirit against the flesh: and these are contrary the one to the other: so that ye cannot do the things that ye would. But if ye be led by the Spirit, ye are not under the law*". (KJV).

To live a spirit filled life we must be guided by the Holy Spirit. It will not force itself on any man or woman. It should be our desire to fulfill the last command of Christ before he ascended into heaven that we are to be witnesses for Him.

How then can we be witnesses for him in a dark and evil world? When our minds and our eyes are consumed with bad news and tragedy on every hand; trying to see the good in so much bad. We can look at the evil days as a good time for believers to boldly proclaim the Gospel of Jesus Christ and share the good news of salvation to the non-believers. There are a multitude of opportunities where we can share the message of Jesus. We should be relentless in our pursuit of saving the unsaved. Although the days are evil and darkness prevails, more than we see positivity and light, take heart. *In Times Like These,* we are not to be overcome by evil, but we can be more than conquerors. To be able to live a spirit filled life, means to reach others with the truth about the gospel of Jesus Christ and this gospel gives the believer power to withstand the test of evil.

The Bible speaks of the Second Coming of Jesus Christ. We do not know when this will be, but the book of Revelations tells us of the signs that will be manifested to show us that the days will not be long until he comes again. We should be about our Father's business telling the world that Christ is alive, and he is coming back to receive his children. He will bring with him a heavenly host and we who are believers will be caught up to meet him in the air. *In times Like These*, rest on the assurance that then and only then, believing in the promises of God makes living a spirit filled life seem effortless.

Questions for Consideration

What do you think is the true source of peace?

_____
_____
_____
_____
_____
_____
_____

Have you ever felt perfect? Explain your answer.

_____
_____
_____
_____
_____
_____
_____

List some things that causes you to feel at peace.

_____
_____
_____
_____
_____
_____

Summary

Make the most of the time we have on this earth. Yes, it becomes difficult to live a spirit-filed life. We spend time on frivolous things, and waste time that could be spent on spirituality and Godliness. We please the flesh and the devil. To set ourselves on a better course will require discipline. Reading scripture, going to bible study, and increasing our prayer life. Start small and then gain momentum with each task. We must guard against being overtaken by the world. The Bible tells us what is necessary to living a spirit-filled life. In it, we will find the toolkit to hammer out a life filled with joy.

Prayer

Lord, keep us in perfect peace.
Help us to remember to pray every day.
Help us to remember to walk in your spirit.
Let us be mindful to study your word, daily.
Help us to surrender all to you. Amen

— 8 —

Through the Looking Glass

The metaphor of a looking glass coined by Cooley (1902), means seeing a representation of oneself on a reflective surface. This phrase applies to our theme of self-reflection as a means of building on our own spirituality. We all must examine ourselves regularly as though we are looking inwardly through an outward source into ourselves by mirrored reflection. How does looking through a looking glass assist us when using our spirituality to help ourselves?

The Bible speaks of our spirituality in the books of Galatians, and Romans. Galatians 5: 22 reads, "...But the fruit of the spirit is love, joy, peace, longsuffering, gentleness, goodness, and faith". Likewise, Romans 8:6 reads, "...for to be carnally minded [is] death; but to be spiritually minded [is] life and peace". (KJV).

The Bible speaks of praying in the spirit. What does it mean to pray in the spirit? This statement does not mean to comment on what we say when we are praying, but rather it helps us to know the importance of following the Spirit's guidance to pray for what the spirit leads us to pray for. Spirit-led prayer is important to us as we work to frow stronger in our faith while simultaneously strengthening our weaknesses. Romans 8: 26 (KJV) tells us, "In the same way, the Spirit helps us in our weaknesses".

There are times we are at a loss regarding what to pray for. Even though we are conscious of our needs and wants, we are unable to utter the words or compose our thoughts when we communicate to God. When this happens to us, we should not worry. The Holy Spirit will guide us through the will of God. If we can be patient and shut out the noise of the world. It helps to look in the looking glass. See your reflection of yourself. See that you are fearfully and wonderfully made in the image of God. While standing there, being silent, ask God to speak to you. Do not rush the process. Sometimes God's love is quiet and slow. It is always there. Just remember, the looking glass gives you a visual representation of your physical self. You are so much more than the outer shell that you and others know you by.

In Times Like These when you do not have words to utter, ask the Spirit to intercede for you. Some of our worries, trials and tribulations might be immediate, others have been ongoing for a prolonged period. How do you ascertain which problem to try and tackle first? None of us have had the right words or always taken the right actions. We are imperfect human beings. We can call on God and others when the going gets rough and every day seems like you are fighting an uphill battle. The Spirit will come and minister to us if only we ask. Let us not underestimate the power of asking for help from our brothers and sisters in Christ. There are others that can give us solace during difficult times.

Let us begin to use the power that is within us to solve both small and large situations that plague us. In times like these, look in the mirror and speak your healing and help into existence. Sometimes you must encourage yourself (Lawrence, 2007). There is so much power in our spoken words. We forget to use the powerful instrument, the tongue, to speak good over our own lives. State your resolve in the looking glass and declare by the spirit that you will overcome bereavement, divorce, friend, job loss, and loss of membership from a church. Declare by the spirit that you will come out on the other side victoriously.

It is during uncertain times that we should look at our own reflection in the mirror and profess to God, "I have your living spirit within me. I claim victory over my circumstance (s). I will use my spirituality to help myself as I know that you will abide in me and with me through this trial". So often we judge our circumstance against others' situation. We look at what they did and judge for ourselves how successful they have been at solving their problems. There is no way to know what another has done to overcome whatever obstacles they faced. Maybe they fasted and prayed.

Maybe they asked the Holy Spirit to help them. We just do not know. We only know the part they tell us, and what we have observed with our own eyes. Be careful not to pattern yourself after others. For their lives are their own. No one but God knows the inner workings of a man or woman's life. Remember that you are unique and so is your life and your life circumstances.

Questions for Consideration

When you look through the looking glass, what do you see?

_____

_____

_____

_____

_____

_____

_____

Do you like what you see?

_____

_____

_____

_____

_____

_____

_____

How has your reflection changed over the years?

_____

_____

_____

_____

_____

_____

What part has spirituality played in your reflection of self?

_____

_____

_____

_____

_____

_____

_____

Summary

Spend time on self-reflection. Do not worry about what others are doing or try to find fault in them. Let us examine our own lives to see where we need to improve. I Corinthians 11: 28-29 states, "But let a man examine himself, and let him eat of the bread and drink of the cup. For he who eats and drinks in an unworthy manner eats and drinks judgment to himself, not discerning the Lord's Holy body"(N KJV). God wants us to examine ourselves and not worry so much about what others are doing. We are his unique creation. Although all of us encounter challenges and distractions, these trials are ours. To maintain our spiritual focus and spiritual well-being, let us appreciate our uniqueness. Anytime you wish to be like someone else ask yourself, "who would I be if I was not trying to be a replica of another person?"

Prayer

Call on the lord because he is ever near to us.
Draw near with faith.
Inspire me to appreciate that I am fearfully and wonderfully made.
Quench my desire to be a carbon copy of anyone else.
Satisfy me with the thought that I am enough
Just as I am.
May God rescue us from ourselves. Amen

— 9 —

Be not Beguiled by
False Prophets

Many will come claiming to be the one true God.

In today's world there are many religious teachings and doctrines. If we are not careful, we will be caught up in the glitz and glamour of a new fad. Be careful to observe with a discerning head and heart, lest you be deceived and follow them. False prophets deceive others by false teachings and present these falsehoods on a platter of attractive fruits and sound bites that are pleasing to the eyes and ears. It may seem hard to distinguish the truth when lies are so enticing and wrapped in a tiny smidgen of truth; intertwined just enough to make one question what they know to be true. Remember, false prophets know the word of God just as well as we do. How else would they be able to trick us into believing their narrative is the truth?

The Bible gives us spiritual radar on how to detect false prophets. Be on guard for these attributes: (1) love of power and themselves. They will not let go of power and will hold on to it at any cost. A false prophet uses relationships to abuse others. Their sole purpose in developing any relationships at all are for the sole purpose of gaining more control over as many people as possible. False prophets do not want anyone else to have any limelight, accolades, or gain any knowledge. They wish to cripple others rather than empower them. (2) False prophets do not like to be corrected.

When criticism is given, they respond with anger. They wish to maintain their authority and will trample anyone and anything that gets in their path. (3) False prophets use emotional blackmail to get what they want.

We all have someone to come to mind when we think of the character of a false prophet. Now that we can recognize one, deciding how to deal with him or her is the next step. In (Deuteronomy 13: 1-18) ESV, tells us how to deal with false prophets when we encounter them. The Bible tells us that these prophets will be and always have been, but do not listen to them when they come with speeches of abandoning the God that you one worshipped. We are instructed to purge ourselves from this evil and cast them out or do not sit and listen to their message. False profits could be those near and dear to you, even in your own household. "Whether they are near to you or as far as the east is from the west, you are not to yield to him, listen to him, look with pity on him, show compassion to him, or even cover up for him. Instead, you are surely to execute him. You must be the first to put him to death with your own hand, and then the hands of the whole community. Stone him to death, because he sought to lure you from the Lord your God, who brought from the land of Egypt, from the land of slavery. Then all Israel will hear about it, be afraid, and will not do this evil thing again among you". (ESV).

God instruct us to do what is right and follow his commandments. If anyone comes preaching anything different, it is a lie. We as believers have been given a spirit of discernment within us. If it does not sound right, feel right, or you know is contrary to what you believe, *In Times Like These,* I say RUN!!!!!!!! Run fast, run far, and keep on running.

Questions for Consideration

Have you encountered false prophets? How were you able to recognize him or her?

_____

_____

_____

_____

_____

_____

_____

Why do you think the tactics of these prophets are so appealing to so many?

_____

_____

_____

_____

_____

_____

_____

Can anything be gained by following the teachings of false prophets?

_____

_____

_____

_____

_____

_____

Summary:

False prophets present themselves as experts on scripture. Be careful that you are not deceived. They twist the scriptures to suit their own agendas. If you do not know God's word for yourself, you will be blinded to the truth of what God wants for us. In the book of Matthew 7:15 (KJV), Jesus warns the disciples of false prophets. He warned them about those who claimed to be prophets and those claiming to be the Messiah. We must be diligent; knowing who speaks what is true and who deviates from the divinely inspired word of God. We must assess the Spirit.

In the latter days, there will be those claiming to be prophets and declare that they speak in the name of the Lord. If the professed prophet speaks in the name of the Lord, and their word does not come true, it is a word that that the Lord has not spoken.

Know this, when we come to the end of the journey of life, we will be held accountable for knowing the truth, we cannot blame anyone else. The Bible has been given to us; everything we need to live by. How will you know the truth when it is spoken if you do not know what is in the book? I would not take the chance of being ignorant of its contents.

Prayer

Dear Lord, keep us grounded in your word.
Keep us grounded in grace and faith in you alone
Help us to stay focused on your truth. Amen.

— 10 —

Spiritual Warfare

"Be alert and of a sober mind. Your enemy the devil prowls
Around like a roaring lion looking for someone to devour.
Resist him, standing firm in the faith, because you know.
That the family of believers throughout the world is
Undergoing the same kind of sufferings."
1 Peter 5: 8-9

We are in a war. We battle every day. Webster defines a war as two factions fighting against each other over a disagreement of some sort. We play a tug of war against good and evil the minute we open our eyes and take our first conscious morning breath. Surely, Christians are under attack. This is not earth-shattering news, for it has been this way for quite some time. Although we at times cannot see our attacker with our physical eyes, we know the enemy is there and we must arm ourselves with the necessary gear to be ready for battle.

Why try to fight something that you cannot see? If you have this defeatist attitude, you have already lost the battle. When we succumb to this attitude when we look at the mess this world is in, this apathetic mentality transfers to our physical realm. Regardless of what we think, there is a spiritual war raging. We will either be swallowed up and defeated by the enemy or we will be the victors over principalities that are unseen.

What does spiritual warfare look like? Where is the battle fought? This world that we live in is a hard and cruel one. Who has time or the capacity to think about a world we cannot see? We must believe in what we cannot see; this is where our faith comes from. Just as there is the tendency to dispel what we cannot see. If we close our minds to spiritual warfare, then we can pretend that it does not exist. Whether we believe it or not does not change the fact that we encounter spiritual warfare around every corner. It lurks like the boogie man under our bed or in our closets, and basements. It jumps out at us at the most inopportune time.

The Bible gives us scripture to let us know that there is another realm that is not visible to us, yet we believe that it exists. Just as we cannot see Jesus Christ, yet we believe. The same principle can apply to our belief in spiritual warfare. Trust and believe that principalities are at work 24-7 to try and destroy every one of us. They stay up late at night devising schemes to make sure that *we live our worst life.*

Do not be naive or ignorant. Unseen demonic forces are very real. There is evil all around us. This evil is where spiritual warfare comes from. Ephesians 6: 12 (KJV) states, "For *we wrestle not against flesh and blood, but against principalities, against powers, against the rulers of the darkness of this world, against spiritual wickedness in high places".* There you go, do not take my word for it. The Bible states it in black and white.

Not all our warfare is fought in the dark. The enemy does move against us in ways that we can see with our physical eye. We witness the way the world is today. For example: the war that rages on in Afghanistan, the killing of innocent children in Uvalde, Texas, the killing of medical personnel in a Dallas hospital maternity ward. I could go on for days listing the evil that has been perpetrated against mankind. These treacherous ats seem random. However, at the very core of these actions are people possessed by demonic forces that feel justified in their actions. With all the occurrences that take place in the world that negatively affect us, we could easily question whether God is still with us. The wicked seem to prosper while the faithful suffer. Be patient, this is only for a little while.

We see the church membership diminishing and seeming to be losing faithful followers. This should not deter the faithful from forging on. The enemy would have us to believe that we do not need church anymore. Certainly, there is no need to assemble in a house of worship because we can view services on Facebook and YouTube. Yes, going to a church building does not make you any more spiritual than the next person, but we are to assemble with one another and be of one accord. There is something immensely powerful that happens when we assemble and worship God; almost magical that cannot be experienced from the sofa at home.

Sometimes, Christians are mocked for our beliefs. The wicked prosper in material things while at times we have little. They often wonder and ask us, "why are you struggling, does not the God you profess to believe in care about you? Where has all this praying and believing gotten you?" It is tempting to question your own belief system when you are going through rough patches. Who are we to be tempted? Jesus himself was tempted in the wilderness. The gospel of Luke 4: 1-13 recounts the story. This account is an example of spiritual warfare. Jesus being full of the Holy Spirit left the Jordan and was led by the Spirit into the wilderness. For forty days, the devil tempted him. He had nothing to eat for forty days, and you can imagine that his human side was hungry. The devil said to him, "if you are the son of God, tell this stone to become bread. Jesus answered, "It is written Man shall not live on bread alone".

As mere mortals we should be expected to experience spiritual warfare. *In Times Like These*, remember what the Bible teaches us, "the little that a righteous man hath is better than the riches of many wicked," (Psalms 37: 16) KJV. The riches that we may envy possessed by the wicked are theirs for a fleeting moment. Meanwhile, the righteous shall inherit the land and dwell therein forever (29). To me that is good news. It is better to be certain that if we are children of God, we shall be upheld in these evil days and receive salvation. Conversely, the wicked shall be cut off. We should trust in the Lord until the end for our reward will be great.

Jesus reminds us in Matthew 28:18 (KJV) that, *"All authority has been given to Me in heaven and on earth."* The war has already been won. Jesus Christ has fought on our behalf. By knowing and being in a relationship with Jesus Christ, we have the victory every day. As the Psalmist stated, "I will lift up mine eyes unto the hills, from whence cometh my help. My help cometh from the Lord, which made heaven and earth", 121: 1-2 (KJV).

Questions for Consideration

Are you fighting a spiritual war? How does it look and feel?

_____

_____

_____

_____

_____

_____

_____

What are your plans for claiming victory over the war?

_____

_____

_____

_____

_____

_____

_____

How will you know that you have won?

_____

_____

_____

_____

_____

_____

_____

Summary

Spiritual warfare is real. Try to fight against demons by yourself and you will surely fail. We must put on the whole armor of God to win the victory. There is a spiritual war taking place in the hearts and minds of humankind. The one would have us turn away from God and serve him. In order for this to happen, we must allow evil to take a foothold in our hearts. How are we to guard against being consumed by the war between good and evil? We must first recognize that spiritual warfare exist. After this, reject the lies that Satan tries to convince us that is true. We must fight the evil that tries to overcome us. One way of fighting is through prayer. Have confidence in knowing that God's power is stronger than anyone or anything that seeks to destroy us.

There is spiritual warfare taking place in the hearts and minds of humanity. The evil one would have us turn away from God and serve him instead. For us to even think of serving the devil, we must allow the devil to assume residence in our hearts; there he gains a foothold. How are we to guard against being consumed by the war between good and evil? We must first recognize that spiritual warfare exist. After this recognition, reject the lies that the devil tries to convince us is the truth.

We must consciously fight the evil that tries to overcome us. Prayer is the most useful weapon we have in our arsenal. Next, we must have confidence in knowing that God's power is stronger than anyone or anything that seeks to destroy us.

Prayer

Today, I put on the whole armor of God.
I claim victory over the enemy.
I join with others in prayer.
That we may intercede for all. Amen.

—11—

Dancing with Wolves
in Sheep's Clothing

Beware of False Prophets, which come to you
in sheep's clothing, but inwardly they are ravening wolves.
Matthew 7:15

According to Project Hero,(N.D.), wolves represent fear and danger. Our society is responsible for this view of wolves. Did you know that wolves also symbolize strong intelligence, the desire for freedom, family, and friendship, and are even a warning sign of threats or lack of trust in others or yourself? (Project Hero, N.D.).

Praise be to God that we have Jesus as our shepherd, and we are his flock. The good shepherd watches out for us. We are called his sheep just as a metaphor to mean that we are Christ's followers. Wolves often want to get amid the sheep and chase them even until death. According to Raisanen, (2014) the basic imagery grew more intensified since the world is the symbol of Pagan Rome's founding, the culture in which Jesus lived and preached. It was not long before the wolf became the symbol of evil, a threat to those in Christ's flock.

Since the wolves move around us freely; sometimes without detection, it is as though they dance in and out of our lives all the time. Most of us dance or have danced in the past. We recognize a dance as a movement that is symbolized as a give and take of a physical nature that requires two or more people; only occasionally one dances alone as in a solo performance or at a recital. The visual picture conjured up is of two people in sync moving harmoniously to the same rhythm at the same time. Usually people are in unison, connected and are on one accord. Seldom are dancers at odds with one another. Although this is a generalization, the statement is more often true than false.

Wolves do not intend to dance with us harmoniously. The Bible cautions us to be aware of those who cause division and create obstacles that are not in line with the ways of God. We should avoid interaction with these types of individuals at all costs. We must be careful of people who flatter us with their lips and try to butter us up. Listen to their words and look at their actions. Their lips drip with words of deceit and their hearts burn with malice and contempt toward others. They have mastered the art of disguising themselves as followers of Christ when all the while they are lovers of men. Yet, within their souls, they are like Satan and the light of God does not shine within them.

At one time, we may find ourselves caught up in their web of deceit. Wolves seem innocent, but all the while they have motives up their sleeves. They disguise their real intentions by camouflaging tactics such as back-biting, maligning our good name, manipulating others to cause them to believe untruths about us, to only advance their own agenda. Wolves strive to do what pleases them at all costs at the expense of others. *In Times Like These, we* wonder how to escape their snare. The Bible cautions us to pray to God for help and guidance. Do not be judgmental of those who want to be seen by men as being followers of Christ. God will judge them for all their deeds done in their bodies. Do not worry about them getting what they deserve, God will take care of them.

The wicked will be cut down in due time. When you have been wounded by wolves in sheep's clothing, do not be ashamed or feel as though you should have known better than to be led down the path of deceit. We are taught to forgive those who despitefully use us and spread falsehoods about us and scandalize our name. *In Times Like These*, know that God is the regulator. He rectifies all wrongs that are perpetrated against us in our earthly bodies.

To be sure, we will encounter wolves in sheep's clothing in every occupation. Wolves disguise themselves in sheep's clothing and deceive themselves into thinking they can hide from God. Do they not know that

Christ the shepherd watches over his sheep? They may sting us for a little while, but our joy comes in the morning time.

Questions for Consideration

Have you been wounded by wolves in sheep's clothing? Explain your answer.

_____

_____

_____

_____

_____

_____

_____

How were you able to escape their snare?

_____

_____

_____

_____

_____

_____

What does it mean if the wolves keep coming after you?

_____

_____

_____

_____

_____

_____

Summary

The meaning of the idiom, "wolves in sheep's' clothing" means that someone is trying to hide their identity. A wolf in sheep's clothing is not a godly person and at their very core is evil and mischief in their hearts.

One way to detect these types of people is to listen to them boast about how much they do and give to others. If they do good works to be seen by men, this behavior does not glorify God. We would be wise to stay clear of these wolves but pray for them that they might cease being hypocrites. Remember the old saying, you are judged by the company you keep. How unfortunate for wolves. They spend so much time trying to hurt others that they end up hurting themselves. Wolves will always be exposed and ousted from among the herd of sheep.

Prayer

Lord open our eyes to see the wolves in sheep's clothing
Help us to recognize those who sow discord repeatedly
Help us to be watchful for our naïve brothers and sisters
Save them from the wrath of the smooth dancing wolves. Amen.

— 12 —

Spiritual Bondage

The Holy Spirit reveals God's truth to us. Jesus explained:
When the Guide you into all truth, for he will not speak on his own
authority, but whatever he hears he will speak,
and he will declare to you the things that are to come.
(John 16:13) ESV

According to Question of the Week (2022), the exact phrase *spiritual bondage* does not appear in the Bible. Scriptures speak of unbelievers' being in bondage to sin (Acts 8:23, KJV) *"For I perceive that thou art in the gall of bitterness, and in the bond of iniquity.* Romans 6:6 KJV states, *"knowing this, that our old man is crucified with him, that the body of sin might be destroyed, that henceforth we should not serve sin."* We also find in 2 Peter 2:19 *"While they promise them liberty, they themselves are the servants of corruption: for of whom man overcome, of the same is he brought in bondage"* (KJV).

Even though the phrase spiritual bondage is not explicitly spelled out in the Bible, its meaning can be inferred to mean that we practice sin. How do we become slaves to sin? When we give the devil an inch and he takes a foot and sets up residence in our lives. What holds us back from being free from sin; for God has promised us to be free from sin. Could our earthly desires be the cause of our remaining in bondage? What do we delight in most and derive pleasure from? We are unable to break the chains of spiritual bondage; God can, however, release us from these chains. When we are in the right relationship with Him, He will give us the desires of our hearts. He will only give us what he knows we need. God cares for his children and reveals the truth in us if we trust and obey him. In due time we come to recognize that our desires are not what he knows is right for us; rather they are wants rather than needs. We should cast every care upon Him and unburden ourselves with things we do not have the power to change.

He can give us spiritual peace that helps us to overcome some of the bondage situations we find ourselves. We are often bound to worldly things that we deem as necessities to our wellbeing; cars, clothes, drugs, liquor, prestige, sex, sports- We derive pleasure from possessing these things. We even find ourselves bound to and worrying about things rather than experiencing the peace that only God can give through the Holy Spirit, which helps us to act in purposeful and effective ways.

We worry about not having enough and we strive to get more of what we already have. Worrying is a part of human nature. We will not stop worrying. Be concerned about things of course, but do not worry because we cannot change anything by our own powers. However, a change of frame of reference will help us. We need only to turn our hearts to faith in God, even when the direst circumstances have pierced our hearts and souls. God has a plan for our lives. There is no need to continue to be slaves to our cars, clothes, houses, jobs, liquor, sex and sports or prestige.

We have forgotten about one of our weapons to overcome bondage. Fasting and praying is not talked about much anymore except at certain times of the year when some participate in the Daniel fast as congregations. Our forebears and foremothers practiced this ritual for many things. For example: they fasted and prayed for their finances, over illnesses and for God to grant them revelations about certain situations they were experiencing. They possessed unshakable faith that at the end of their fasting and praying, God would answer their prayers and grant them every one of their petitions.

We are very different and many years, even decades beyond our forefathers and foremother's lifetimes. Times have changed, but many of the old rituals were tried and true. The older generation relied on their faith and searched scripture to guide them in their practices. Fasting is a way of humbling ourselves before God. Psalms 35: 13, KJV, reads "But as for me, when they were sick, my clothing was sackcloth: I humbled my soul with fasting; and my prayer returned into my own bosom". The Israelites wore sackcloth as a sign of humbleness and submission before God. We are long past the days of wearing sackcloth. We can never be beyond the need for fasting and praying to break the chains that keep us spiritually in bondage.

Bondage and sin are linked to one another. If you used to sin and you have repented and stopped sinning, good for you. We are our own worst enemy. Know that God has forgiven you for past sins. Break free from the mindset of unforgiveness and move on; do not hang on to feelings of doubt and worthlessness about yourself. Others may remind you of how you sinned. *In Times Like These*, look around and see if they can add one day to your life, put one hair on your head, or add one cubit to your stature. Stop worrying about other people so much when it comes to our forgiveness and focus more on our one-to-one relationship with God.

Living in self unforgiveness is a sure way that the devil can take a foothold in your life. If you allow it, you will remain in spiritual bondage. *In Times Like These*, realize that it is possible to be free from bondage. Everything we need to know about breaking free of the chains that binds us is in the Bible. Ephesians 1:3 (KJV) reads, *"Blessed be the God and Father of our Lord Jesus Christ, who hath blessed us with all spiritual blessings in heavenly places in Christ,"*

As children of God, we possess all spiritual blessing there are. All we need to do to receive these blessings is to pray without ceasing, confess our sins because he is faithful to forgive us, and humble ourselves before the Lord.

We should always rejoice in the Lord. Keep praises continually in your heart and in your mouth. Do not allow spiritual bondage to keep you from enjoying a life of freedom. To live a life free from bondage may not be that easy. Just remember, God has given us everything that we need to break free from sin and doubt. Dr. Anthony Evans has written in his newly released book, *Discover Your Destiny.*

Questions for Consideration

Are you holding on to past sins? Why or why not?

_____

_____

_____

_____

_____

_____

_____

Do others keep reminding you of past sins? How have you managed this?

_____

_____

_____

_____

_____

_____

How often do you practice fasting and praying? What have been your results?

_____

_____

_____

_____

_____

_____

Summary

Spiritual bondage is anything that keeps us from being committed to God. As Christians, we can find ourselves in bondage just as non-believers can. Often, we have lived in a particular sin for so long, we feel unworthy of forgiveness by God. We hold on to the feelings of guilt about what was done in the past, while God has long ago thrown our transgressions in the sea of forgiveness.

Never forget that we are all sinners saved by grace. We must not yield to temptation, but when we do, ask God to help us. Seek the Lord and resist the devil.

Prayer

Heavenly Father help us to submit to you.
Let us draw near to you.
Cleanse our hands and purify our hearts. Amen.

— 13 —

Do Not Fret

Fret not thyself of evildoers, neither thou be envious
Against the workers of iniquity. For they shall soon
Be cut down like the grass, and wither as the
green herb
(Psalms 27: 1-2). KJV

The meaning of the word *Fret* is derived from the old English language. It means "to consume" or worry unnecessarily (Old Oxford English Dictionary, 2014). It is difficult to see the Lord's hand at work during the evil days in which we live. If we allow our fretful minds to overtake us, no good can come of it. Our physical eyes and limited mental capacity find it hard to comprehend spiritual things. Satan would have us to believe that the Lord has abandoned us.

We fret over so many things. We wonder what we will eat, wear, fret for the sake of fretting. We fret over our children, running out of milk, too few bottles of water, gas prices, food prices, the weather, conference claims for church, friendships, or lack thereof. We can make up things to fret about; the list is limitless. We fret over what others have that we do not have but would like to possess. Some fret over the church and its direction and lack of spiritual growth and declining membership. What are we able to change by mere fretting endlessly?

The bible tells us to fret not. God's righteousness will be upheld even in these evil days. Wickedness will not prevail. For the wicked and wickedness will be cut off. We should still trust in the Lord until the end for our reward will be great.

Psalms 37: 7 (KJV) tells us,"

> "Rest in the Lord and wait patiently for him.
> Fret not thyself because of him who prospered in his way,
> because of the man who bringeth wicked
> devices to pass."

The righteous shall receive salvation and the wicked shall be cut off. We should trust in the Lord. It cannot be repeated enough. Not fretting is easier said than done. For example: your child is sick, and you worry. The doctors are doing all that they can to try and make them better. Our human nature causes us to worry. Even the Christian still worries.

In times Like These ask God to give you strength. There is no shame in asking for help. Some burdens are too hard to bear alone. Another example would be when there is a false rumor started about you. Whether the rumor is true or false, some people delight in idle gossip and will listen to the rumor; not caring about the truth of the information. You desperately try to defend your good name against slander. Is it not better to hold your peace? Something my late grandmother would always say, "hold your peace." It is difficult, but soon the liar will be found out. Most reasonable people see a troublemaker for who they truly are and use their own intelligence to decipher for themselves the truth of the matter.

Stop fretting over any and everything. Do we not trust God to fight on our behalf? Where has our faith in God gone? We walk around constipated with worry and fear. How are we to survive? For on any given day something irregular may happen to us. We cannot continue to live our lives hoping for a life that shields us from all hurt and danger. No such life exists. Even Jesus suffered trials and tribulations and we will continue to do so. How we manage the trials is what is important.

According to (Killough, 2022) there are seven ways we can cope with trials and tribulations of life. One way among the seven ways is to pray specifically to God. "That's why, when we ask of Him something specific that we believe is the answer to our problem, we need to also ask for faith, patience, wisdom, endurance, courage and hope."

Questions for Consideration

What do you fret about?

_____

_____

_____

_____

_____

_____

_____

When we fret, is it because we feel alone? Explain your answer.

_____

_____

_____

_____

_____

_____

_____

When you are feeling anxious, what or who relieves your anxiety?

_____

_____

_____

_____

_____

_____

_____

How have you managed being the subject of a lie?

_____
_____
_____
_____
_____
_____
_____
_____

Were you vindicated? If so, how did it make you feel?

_____
_____
_____
_____
_____
_____

Summary

Because we are human beings, made of flesh and blood, we have the tendency to worry about situations that arise. Even in challenging times, we must submit our ways to the Lord. Even during trials and pain, give thanks anyhow. When we give thanks and praise to God, we view our circumstances through a better lens. One that is more uplifting to us.

Prayer

Lord help us to remain at peace.
Help us to not fret.
Let us remember our petitions and praise.
helps to lift us up. Amen

— 14 —

God Hears our Cries: Praise Amid Despair

Beloved if our heart does not condemn us,
We have confidence before God.
And whatever we ask we receive from him,
Because we keep his commandments and do
What pleases him, (I John 3: 21-22, ESV)

D o you ever wonder why terrible things happen to good people? Do you wonder why a loving God lets bad things happen to you or someone you love? We have suffering because of the sin of fallen man. God allows trials to come in our lives to test our faith. When we are faced with difficult situations and we overcome the situation, it proves to make us stronger. When the next trial arises, we are poised to seek God's help with the anticipation that his Grace is sufficient to meet all our needs.

Staying tuned in to God is how we ask for help and at the same time, give him praises for what he has already done for us. One way of communicating with God is through prayer. There are many scriptures in the Bible that speak to God hearing our prayers when we cry out to him.

For example, a list of two such scriptures can be found below:

1. "He regards the prayer of the destitute and does not despise their prayer", Psalms 102: 17 (ESV).
2. "Do not be anxious about anything, but in everything by prayer and supplication with Thanksgiving let your requests be known to God", Philippians 4: 6 (ESV).

We all face devastating situations in our lives. Some devastating situations are death of a loved love, loss of employment, divorce, and other tragedies. This conscious effort to forge onward in spite of the challenges we face, is a testament to our faith. However, forging onward is easier said than done.

We can all tell stories of times we were in despair, yet we praised the Lord amid the challenge we faced. I remember when our son left us to go home to be with the Lord at an early age. None of us felt much like praising God, but we did it just the same. We praised him for each of our lives, our son's life, our daughters' lives. We praised him for everything that we could think of that He still allowed us to have. We listened to God to guide us through the maze of a myriad of emotions during the darkest season of our lives. We cried out to him in our despair, and He heard our cries. He guided our footsteps daily. Had it not been for the Lord on our sides, we would have lost our minds. We are still standing only because of his mercy towards us.

Our story is just one of many. We sometimes lose our direction amid trials. God steps in and provides the spiritual compass that leads us to him to hold on to a lifeline when we feel we are in deep water about to drown. We all have testaments to how God has brought us through tremendous trials. My family can attest to our spiritual walk being strengthened even more after enduring such horrific and unimaginable circumstances.

Allow me to introduce you to my friend Cindy. Cindy is what people would refer to as a nice person. She is neat in appearance, clothes clean and well fitted, hair trimmed and glossy, an overall well-groomed individual. She is especially cordial to all she meets. She keeps her home, children, and surroundings very tidy. If you look further into the world in which Cindy lives behind closed doors, you will see many cracks in an otherwise ordinary façade. You see, Cindy survived two strokes at an early age. She is also a survivor of a near fatal heart attack. Cancer once consumed her body and she beat that too. If that was not enough, Cindy has a special needs son who she cared for mainly by herself because her husband worked out of town. You would think that Cindy does not have a care in the world. She never stopped attending church services, praising God, helping others in need by calling on the phone, visiting the sick, giving food and clothing to the needy and hungry. Unless she told you her story, you would not know she had survived such trials.

If you watch Cindy closely at church, you see the passion she displays for her praise to God. Certainly, she has much to despair about; but she gives unadulterated praise to the Almighty amidst any despair she may be going through. Cindy will tell you that she has cried out to God on so many occasions during her hours of distress and He heard her cries She will tell you that she has a newfound sense of spirituality and connection to the Holy Spirit. It is as though she has been healed and called to do a greater work for the Lord than most people.

If Cindy's story was not illuminating enough about how God answers our cries during despair, I will tell you the story of another friend named Joan. Joan is older than Cindy but has some of the same physical attributes. She was neat in appearance, soft spoken, and friendly toward others. Although Joan had not suffered many medical problems herself, just like Cindy, her nuclear family and extended family have seen many dark days. Joan is the product of a God-fearing family, reared in the church, sings in the choir, a well-respected person on the job and in the community where she lives. By all accounts she appears to have lived a good life.

Once the layers have been peeled back on Joan's life, you see she has suffered physical abuse at the hands of her husband. If you looked closely, you could see the heavy foundation makeup she used to camouflage the bruises on her arms and under her eyes. Joan typically wears high heels, but on days it is hard for her to walk because of the beating she has suffered, she wears flat shoes.

Those of us who were close to her learned to read the signs of a very turbulent she had endured. During the many trials that Joan confronted during the relationship with her abusive spouse, she never lost her faith and never neglected to give God praise. She stated that God loved her, and she knew that He would never abandon her. She first cried out to God to save her from such a treacherous relationship. After many years of pleading with God, she herself will tell you, she felt the Holy Spirit guiding her to new heights of oneness with the Father. Her prayers then changed from God deliver me from this tumultuous relationship to God help me to summon the courage and provide for me the means to leave. For she knew God had better plans for her.

I in no way advocate for a spouse to remain in an abusive relationship. Each couple has their own dynamics, and each person must do what is best for them at the time. Just know that God did not make male or female to suffer under the hands of another human being. *In Times Like These*, if you experience what these women have experienced or know someone who has gone through or is suffering similar circumstances, exercise spiritual fortitude to get through the rough times. Reach out to God on their behalf; we should not be stingy with our prayers for others.

Just as this family and these two women were able to praise God while they were going through trials in their lives, we too can find peace during moments of despair. We can praise God during unbearable circumstance. Remember Christ died such a horrible death that we might live. No amount of suffering that we face can come close to the sacrifice that he made for us. Yet he praised his heavenly Father even at the hour of his death. Have enough faith to believe that God hears you and he will answer your prayers. Always remember that the Holy Spirit was sent to be comforter to us. If we make the conscious effort to connect to our spirituality, it can help us to overcome insurmountable situations.

Questions for consideration

Have you managed and/or are you managing moments of despair that have come or are present in your life?

_____

_____

_____

_____

_____

_____

_____

What has been your outcome?

_____

_____

_____

_____

_____

_____

_____

How have you helped someone else deal with moments of despair in his/her life?

_____

_____

_____

_____

_____

_____

_____

Summary

The Lord has a way of testing our metal. It is easy to praise Him when everything is going well for us. Conversely, in times of despair we lose sight of God and focus more on our circumstances. Psalms 42 (KJV) speaks to praising God in the midst of being downcast. We are unable to restore ourselves to the right spirit. Our miseries will overtake us, but we need only to cry out to the Lord and he will rescue us.

Prayer

I need to know that you care that you love me, be my refuge from pain, replacing my distress with peace, and be my strength when I feel weak and find it hard to carry on. Help me not to fear the future but to boldly trust that you are in control when my emotions plunge me down, and when I am in despair. Amen (Taken from Prayers for Difficult Times, Mission Australia).

— 15 —

Like Stars in the Galaxy

"And God said, let us make man in our image, After our likeness."
(Genesis 1:26) KJV

Each of us is unique. We may share the same DNA of our parents and siblings, but we can be distinguished by our unique fingerprints. Even identical twins do not share the same fingerprint even though they were made by the same fertilized egg. We are fearfully and wonderfully made by our creator. Knowing that no two humans are alike should give us pause; stop comparing ourselves to one another.

Not only are we one of a kind, but a child born over 2,000 years ago in Bethlehem was one of a kind. He was one of a kind in his immaculate conception. He was one of a kind in his virgin birth, He was one of a kind in his sinless Son of God (for every human is born a sinner). He is one of a kind because he alone died for us and his death reconciled humans to the Father, Acts 4:12 (KJV) reads, "There is salvation in no one else' for there is no other name under heaven that has been given among men by which we must be saved." We then, being made in His likeness, can take delight in the fact that we are a walking unique creation, to the bank.

We are like stars in the galaxy. God flung these stars into the heavens on the fourth day of creation and only he can call each one by name. We forget that all of us have a purpose in life that is unique to us. Some never live out their purpose on this earth. The cemetery is full of people with unfulfilled life purposes. What we do, are, and accomplish in this life, is not our own creation. It is God fulfills his purpose through us. We are mere vessels through which he performs his work.

Are you envious of what someone else has? Do you long for a lean muscular figure, the gift of oration? Are you covetous of your neighbor's house, or wife and children? Are you angry because you were passed over for a promotion you felt should have been given to you? At times we feel that we are living a marginal life while others are sailing through on easy street. STOP IT! Each of us was made to fulfill a unique purpose in life. If we allow the Holy Spirit to guide us in the direction of our life's purpose, we too can shine like the stars in the galaxy. None of us has the same preordained purpose. We are only seeing with our limited mind's eye. Although our perception is real to us, there is always a back story to another's success to which we are not privy. We do not know the inner workings of another man or woman's story.

Instead of being consumed by envy and jealousy, be happy for our brothers and sister's good fortune. In time, God will grace us with His favor if we open ourselves up to him. Rest assured that what God has for us is for us. The whole world moves at the direction of God. He cares more for mankind than he does any other creation. We are like stars in the galaxy. Every star is different, but each one shines as bright as the other and all-stars light our path at night, not just some stars. Not one of us can change someone else or our God given purpose, whether we develop it or not, by what we wish for. Almighty God has worked everything out in advance, even down to the place where we will spend eternity with him.

Our resting place is unique to us. Our heavenly Father has prepared many mansions for us all. He did not prepare just one for everybody. Unlike clones, He wants us to be different and has given us different talents. Would you want to be a cookie-cutter version of someone else? How boring is that? Even our spirituality is unique to each one of us. We convey this spirituality in the way that we practice our gifts and talents. Likewise, the Holy Spirit guides us through the exercising of these gifts. In the Bible, I Corinthians speaks about spiritual gifts. It speaks of spiritual gifts of prophecy, knowledge, wisdom, understanding, counsel, fear of the Lord, and courage. Spiritual gifts are 'spiritual' in nature for they are given by the Holy Spirit to every believer (1Corinthians 12:7-11). Each gift is a manifestation of the Spirit (1

Corinthians 12:7). Spiritual gifts are 'spiritual' in that they are given only to those who are believers in Jesus Christ.

In order not to confuse spiritual gifts with our talents and abilities allow me to draw your attention to some concrete expressions of other forms of gifts and talents that are given to humans and are more commonly recognizable to us all. This is not an exhaustive list by any means, but you comprehend the idea intended. For example, the gift of caretaking, listening, praying, running, singing, public speaking, and preaching. All our gifts are to be shared; not sat on and they are to be used to the glory of God.

In times when you feel less than, more than, and wish to be in someone else's shoes, realize that your shoes fit you simply fine. Remember you are like a star in the galaxy. So unique that you cannot be duplicated.

Questions for Consideration

What have you recognized as your God given gift/ You may choose from the above list or tell your own. How are others benefitting from the sharing of your gift? Explain your answer.

_____

_____

_____

_____

_____

_____

_____

Have you envied another person for their gift? Do you perceive their gift to be better or less than yours even though the gift is the same? Write about how you overcame that challenge.

_____

_____

_____

_____

_____

_____

_____

Is there a difference between an acquired skill and a God given talent? Explain your answer.

_____
_____
_____
_____
_____
_____
_____

Describe ways in which you use your gift(s) to exercise your spirituality.

_____
_____
_____
_____
_____
_____
_____

How are we like everyone else?

_____
_____
_____
_____
_____
_____

List the attributes that make you unique from all other humans?

_____
_____
_____
_____
_____
_____

Summary

Each of us is a unique creation. It is my belief that Man did not evolve from spontaneous combustion. Psalms 139:13 states, "For it is thou that dist. form my reins. The Lord knitted us in our mother's womb. The Lord knows our innermost thoughts and desires because we are revelations of Himself. Because He is our master architect, our purpose in life should be to serve Him and appreciate His mindfulness of us in all we do.

All of God's thoughts are irrefutably Holy. Because we are made in His image, our knowledge of him and his appreciation for us should propel us to accept that we are like none other. If we meditate on this idea, we begin to put away envy and jealousy of one another. We are just enough the way God made us.

Prayer

God, we thank you for the beauty of our uniqueness
We are blessed to be made in your image
Thank you for the beauty of the earth.
Thank you for the diversity of humankind that we witness every day.
Help us to realize that we are enough.
Your grace is 100% sufficient for us all.
We need not long to be cookie cutter people.
Thank you for giving us all a unique purpose
May we be a shining star to light the way for ourselves and others
We do all this to glorify you.
We pray this prayer in Jesus' name. Amen

— 16 —

Be Strong and Courageous:
Do not be Gripped by Fear

"Be strong and courageous, for the Lord
your God will be with you."
Joshua 1:9 (NKJV)

Perilous times have come to us all and will continue to come if this world continues to exist. *In Times Like These* we question whether we are walking in faith. Wondering have we done wrong. Have we brought calamity on ourselves, family, or friends? Know that these feelings are normal. We are made of flesh and blood and are human. *In Times Like These,* rest upon your faith to undergird you.

We are wrestling with a global pandemic known as COVID-19. It has gripped us all with fear. The fallout from COVID-19 has changed the way we operate at all levels of society. People died and are still dying. Our churches have been closed or drastically restricted attendance. Travel restricted, the way we receive medical care altered, burial of the dead restricted; the world we live in has been forever changed.

As Christians we are taught to be strong and courageous just as Joshua was when he was charged with taking the Israelites across the Red Sea. We are not crossing the Red Sea being chased by Pharoah's army, but it feels like sharks are swimming around us ready to bite off our limbs, halt our enjoyment of leisure activities and yes, pose a threat to our safety and life. We can attest to being frightened of the world and what catastrophic event will befall us next.

Each of us would be hard pressed to find someone that has not been affected by the pandemic in some way. For so long, our country has been able to go about business as usual. Long gone are the days that a massive global pandemic took so many lives at a given point in time. Probably not since the plague of 1924 that started in Los Angeles, California and the Spanish flu of the winter of 1918 has America lost so many people.

We sat with held breaths wondering how to escape the virus and what to do if we contracted it; feeling it was only a matter of time before it engulfed our whole household. Some were lucky enough to have escaped the virus so far. However, the likelihood that we will catch it lurks in the back of our minds.

Having these occasional thoughts does not mean we are not Christians. As Christians we too get frightened of the known and the unknown. What this means is that we are exercising our common sense and taking precautions to try and protect our health and life. What sets us apart or should I say, what should set us apart from non-believers is our hope and faith. *In Times Like These*, others are watching how we rely on our faith to bear our burdens and misfortunes. Some may even wish for us to fall. We must be strong and courageous; immovable steadfast. God's *"got it"* and He has us. Do not conform to what the world says do. We must wait upon the Lord to work out our problems. For in time, we will reap the harvest if we do not give up.

Questions for Consideration

How has the global pandemic affected your spiritual life?

_____

_____

_____

_____

_____

_____

_____

How has your faith journey/spirituality increased/decreased due to the pandemic?

_____

_____

_____

_____

_____

_____

When did you could share your faith during the pandemic?

_____

_____

_____

_____

_____

Summary

"Be strong and courageous. Do not be afraid; do not be discouraged, for the Lord your God will be with you wherever you go," (Joshua 1:9). God is always present with us even when we think he is not there. This verse was an instruction to Joshua to obey all the laws that Moses had given to him. Like Joshua, we are not to be deterred from what God wants us to do.

We should not be double minded about what we are supposed to do. Hold steadfastly to our hope and faith in God even in the midst of a worldwide catastrophe. We must obey all of God's commands. Seek God first, because He gives us our power. Without Him, we can do nothing. Just remember, whatever God promises us, just like he did for the Israelites, he will come through. God is a loving Father and will never abandon us.

Prayer

Lord God, grant us your peace during these trying times.
We call on you heavenly Father to heal our land.
Help us to draw strength from you.
Let us not be afraid.
Teach us to plan and be diligent to protect our lives and our loved ones.
Give us the courage to forge on
When we have lost so much and see so much devastation around us
Grant us the peace in knowing that you will be with us no matter what. Amen

— 17 —

Spirituality Renewed

But those who hope in the Lord will renew their strength.
They will soar on wings like eagles; they will run and not grow weary.
They will walk and not faint.
Isaiah 40: 31(KJV)

A spiritual renewal is a reawakening of our conscious minds on a spiritual level. At a time when we have become hardheaded and stiff necked toward God; it is time to break the chains that have us bound to such spiritual apathy. The spiritual reawakening of which I speak is not the spiritual awakening that is associated with Buddhism, Mindful Zen, or the process of enlightenment per se. When I speak of spiritual renewal, I am speaking of what the book of Ephesians states, "**Ephesians 4:22-24 (KJV),** *"To put off concerning the former conversation the old man, which is corrupt according to the deceitful lusts: And be renewed in the spirit of your mind.*

God has given us the tools we need to get back to where he wants us to be. Given the state of the world we live in, it is time for us to do all we can to redirect ourselves and save our society from total collapse. Sitting and doing nothing will not solve anything. Yes, there are times to be still and see the wonders of the Lord, but most of the mess up in this world is by our own hands. We messed it up so why not try to do what we can to fix things?

We do nothing, then we are destined to continue this path of destruction. Enough is enough. I do not know about you, I want myself, my children, and grandchildren to live in a world that is much better than the one they have now. Let us make the choice to do better and to be better. Change starts with just a few people and from there it catches like wildfire. Before you know it, a spiritual reawakening has become contagious.

There is a better way to live than how we are living. I know because I was witness to it. When I grew up, there was reverence for God and all things pertaining to the Holy Spirit. Non-believers even had respect for those who called themselves religious even if they themselves did not subscribe to any religion. Non-believers would not dare desecrate the church, cemetery, or anything having to do with God. It has become a chaotic situation now. Houses of worship are destroyed, religious implements stolen or desecrated and there are those who would curse a member of the clergy and think nothing of it. Ask yourself, "is this what we are doing, now?"

As for me, I am sick and tired of the same old everything goes. This life that we live on earth is not the end. When we pass through this earthly life, we will begin life anew. However, to gain entrance into the new life we must make some preparations while we live this life on earth. Want to know how to begin a spiritual awakening? I am glad you asked. One way to a spiritual awakening is through fasting and praying as mentioned in an earlier chapter. Prayer is our key to combat the hold that the shadowy world has on us. We are easily blinded by the negativity that plagued the world. The devil would have us throw up our hands and ask," what is the use?"

I come to remind us that there is good in the world. We should spend more time looking for it. Rather than spend so much time in the *woe is me* mindset, be the positive force in your own life and someone else's. Walk in confidence knowing that there is a better way for us all.

We must have faith. A faith just like the Israelites had when they marched around the walls of Jericho for seven days and the walls came tumbling down. They did not know how they were going to fight the battle or get around the wall to fight, but because they were obedient to the commands of their Father, He fought the battle on their behalf. When you find your faith waning, drained of energy, seems to be no way out, forge ahead. The suffering, negativity, and grief will not last always. We must speak positively about our situation. It is not an easy task to overcome discouragement and loss in our lives. At times we feel alone and try to manage the burdens all by ourselves. *In Times Like These*, ask for help from the Father. We should learn to pray for a supernatural spiritual intervention.

WESTSIDE Church in Lewisville, Texas 2018, published a 31 days of prayer brochure. Each day in the month of January scriptures to be read were given and directions on how to fast and pray each day of that month. The Prayer Ministry led the effort. The point is, they expected remarkable things to happen. On the agreement page for the practice of fasting and praying for the month is reads, "EXPECT God to show you great and mighty things… things which you have never seen before."

At one time or the other, each of us has needed to renew our spirituality. The first record of spiritual renewal recorded in the Bible comes from the Book of Luke. This event happened on the day of Pentecost. This account can be found in the book of Acts. To sum up what happened on that day, the Jewish people were having their Spring Festival. It was customary to thank God for the beginning of the agricultural harvest. To sum up what happened; a spiritual awakening and renewal took place; many people that spoke various languages were assembled. On this very day, those assembled could understand each other even though many were speaking in a language that was not their native tongue. The Holy Spirit arrived, and the multitude saw flames of fire, heard roaring winds; thousands were converted. Jesus had promised that the Holy Spirit would come. After witnessing all these occurrences, 3,000 souls were converted after hearing Peter speak on the message of Jesus Christ. The Christian movement began on that day.

Only God can renew us spiritually. First, we must have the desire to be renewed and ask God to renew us. We must believe that he will grant our request. We must tell others about Jesus; we should not be stingy with the Gospel or selfish about our own salvation. When we are sincere about our evangelism and telling others how great God is, the sincerity can be felt by others, and they will know that God is real. During spiritual renewal we can expect four things to take place. First, Christians participate in corporate prayer praying about the same concerns, Second, we are moved to testify to others about Jesus, Third, the church shares the message of Jesus with people from different backgrounds, and fourth, others will be convinced or hostile to your message. You will know that you have experienced spiritual renewal when you are not deterred from your message. Instead, you are further propelled to keep proclaiming the news of Jesus Christ.

We should be concerned about our own spiritual renewal and the renewal of our brothers and sisters. Not only should we pray for ourselves but pray collectively for and with one another praising God for his gift of salvation. When spiritual renewal occurs, there is tremendous joy and peace packaged into one. We burst with confidence that the Holy Spirit has renewed our lackluster spirit. We cannot wait to tell others of what He has done for us.

Questions for Consideration

How does God want us to show love to others?

_____

_____

_____

_____

_____

_____

_____

Why is it important to engage with others that are of different backgrounds than we are to talk about Jesus?

_____

_____

_____

_____

_____

_____

_____

Why are people resistant to the message of Jesus? How do some respond?

_____

_____

_____

_____

_____

_____

Why should Christians participate in corporate prayer?

_____

_____

_____

_____

_____

_____

_____

How do you experience spiritual renewal?

_____

_____

_____

_____

_____

_____

Summary

The present state of our world is a mere repeat of what happened when people rejected the Word of God.

Prayer

*Create in me oh God the **right** spirit.*
*and **renew** the right spirit within me. Amen*

—18—

Discussion

This chapter recaps for readers how to use spirituality and faith to gain confidence and renewed hope in themselves. Activities have been presented to prick the hearts and minds to imagine ways in which all can live in an ever-changing world and foster a brighter future. It is my prayer that this book has elucidated how Christians should behave in times of stress and uncertainty. Hopefully we have found valid ways of reacting to challenges we face and during those challenges learned how to affirm the value of prayer and its significance and importance to connecting with God.

As Christians we must reaffirm our faith and exercise our faith to be in right relationship with God. Only then can our prayers be effectual for ourselves and for others. The recognition that God above hears us at all times and answers our prayers according to his timetable, provides a way of understanding that God can use each of us no matter the shape we are in to further his grand design for our lives. This recognition helps us to see that the creator desires goodness for us that when we falter, we are not lost forever, but relying on the Hoy Spirit and activating our own spirituality is what is required to live a life that is more spirit filled.

We are God's most beloved creation. Our human existence is but a few short years in God's timing. We must work while we are alive for when we cease to exist in this life, there is no more work that a dead man can do. God gives to us time and chances over again to get it right. It is His desire that all of us be saved because He loves us. We can always count on his love. God so loved us that he sent his son to die for us so that we might have eternal life through him and have it more abundantly. God's love is not fickle like ours. It is not dependent on whether we love him back. It last forever and He loves those that hate him. What a mighty God we serve.

Question for Consideration

What was the most valuable lesson you received from reading this study guide?

_____

_____

_____

_____

_____

_____

_____

_____

_____

_____

_____

_____

_____

_____

_____

_____

_____

_____

_____

_____

_____

_____

Prayer

Dear God, thank you for the opportunity to come into your presence.
We come to you with adoration, praise, and thanksgiving in our hearts.
We have all sinned and have come short of relying totally on you.
We ask that you forgive us for all our transgressions
against our brothers and sisters.
Most of all forgive us for our transgressions against you.
Grant us the desire to seek after you.
Help us to be mindful to study your word and govern ourselves accordingly.
Bless those that are in need in any way.
Prick our hearts and minds to want to serve you better.
For we know that we are to be the light of the world
Spreading your message at home and abroad
We pray this prayer in the name of Jesus the Christ. Amen

Epilogue

If we depend on the *Holy Spirit*, God's plan for our lives will be realized. We try to fix our own problems. When our efforts do not give us the desired results, we then seek guidance from the *Holy Spirit*. Our mode of operation should be the opposite. In many circumstances, self-reliance causes us to fail. You can never go wrong relying on the *Holy Spirit* to help you to overcome life's many hurdles.

When we rely on God and the *Holy Spirit* working in us, we grow spiritually, and we act according to what God desires of us. We only can be victorious in this life if we act through the power of God because as mortals we are too weak within our own power to do anything. Oftentimes a make a mess of situations and our lives trying to act within our human power. We must surrender our whole lives to God and let the *Holy Spirit* work within us. Then and only then can we enjoy a life that we are meant to live; one that God ordains.

Glossary

Agape- In the New Testament Greek agape, in the New Testament, the fatherly love of God for humans, as well as the human reciprocal love for God. In Scripture, the transcendent agape love is the highest form of love and is contrasted with eros, or erotic love, and philia, or brotherly love.

Apocalypse-the complete final destruction of the world, as described in the biblical book of Revelation.

Apostasy is the abandonment or renunciation of a religious or political belief.

Beguiled charm or enchant (someone), sometimes in a deceptive way.

Bible -The Bible is a collection of religious texts or scriptures that are held to be sacred in Christ comes from the Greek word (Christos), meaning "anointed one". The word is derived from the Greek verb (chrono), meaning "to anoint." In the Greek Septuagint, was a semantic loan used to translate the Hebrew (, messiah), meaning "[one who is] anointed".

Evil- morally reprehensible: Sinful, Wicked

Faith-complete trust or confidence in someone or something.
strong belief in God or in the doctrines of a religion, based on spiritual apprehension rather than proof.

Falling away- Jesus warned the disciples concerning the final days in Matthew 24:10-12: "At that time many will turn away from the faith and will betray and hate each other, and many false prophets will appear and deceive many people. Because of the increase of wickedness, the love of most will grow cold." These are the characteristics of the great apostasy of the end times.

Fret -are constantly or visibly worried or anxious.

Holy Spirit-The Holy Spirit is referred to as the Lord and Giver of Life in the Nicene creed. He is the Creator Spirit, present before the creation of the universe and through his power everything was made in Jesus Christ, by God the Father.

Intersectionality-the interconnected nature of social categorizations such as race, class, and gender as they apply to a given individual or group, regarded as creating overlapping and interdependent systems of discrimination or disadvantage.

Lectio Divina- Latin for Divine Reading, is a traditional monastic practice of spiritual reading, meditation and prayer.

Narrative-a spoken or written account of connected events; a story.

Pentecost-Pentecost is a Christian holiday which takes place on the 50th day after Easter Sunday. It commemorates the descent of the Holy Spirit upon the Apostles and other followers of Jesus Christ while they were in Jerusalem celebrating the Feast of Weeks, as described in the Acts of the Apostles.

Prick-an act of piercing something with a fine, sharp point.

Spirituality-Traditionally, **spirituality** referred to a religious process of re-formation which "aims to recover the original shape of man", oriented at "the image of God" as ...

Spirit Renewal-To put off your old self, which belongs to your former manner of life and is corrupt through deceitful desires, and to be renewed in the spirit of your minds, and to put on the new self, created after the likeness of God in true righteousness and holiness."

Spiritual Warfare-**Spiritual warfare** is the Christian concept of fighting against the work of preternatural evil forces. It is based on the biblical belief in evil spirits,

Bibliography

Bright, B. (2022) Spiritual Growth. Have you made the wonderful discovery of a spirit-filled life?

Cooley, C. (1902), The Looking Glass Self. New York, Scribner.

DeLashmutt, G. (2008). Arisen Technology Corporation.

Ehmann, Karen, (2019). Fret No Thyself. http://proverbs 31.org/read/devotions/full-post/2019/04/29/fret-not-yourself.

Evans, Dr. Anthony, (2013). Discover Your Destiny: let God use you how he made you. Harvest House Publishers. Eugene, Oregon.

Graham, F. (2012). Good news in these evil days. To the point.

Hall, E. (2020). The covid-19 pandemic tests everyone's spiritual wellbeing, atheists, and believers alike.

Hardy, R. (2022). Losing my religion: The pandemic is causing many to lose faith in God. HEALTH & WELLBEING, New Atlas

Killough, C. (2020). Seven keys to coping with the trials and tribulations of life. https://lifehopeandtruth.com/life/christian-living/seven-keys-to-coping-with-the-trials-and-tribulations-of-life/

Kramer, S. (2022). NPR, All Things Considered. www.npr.org.

Landry, C. (2020). Five ways you can break free from spiritual bondage: Being a doer of the word. https://www.curtlandry.com/5-ways-you-can-break-free-from-spiritual-bondage.

Lawrence, D. (2006). Song, *Encourage Yourself.*

Lewis, R. (2020). Spirituality, not just religion, may be declining. purpose without God.com

Lipka, M. and Gecewicz, C. (2017) More Americans now say they are spiritual but not religious, PEW Research Center, peewreasearch.org.

Mashburn, R. (2020). What does it mean for everything when there is a season? https://www.christianity.com/author/rebecca-mashburn/

Mission Australia (N.A.) Australian Parliament House. https://.aph.gov.au>ho...

Mody, S. (2021). Millennials lead shift away from organized religion as pandemic tests Americans' faith. CNBC

Mueller, C. (2021). One of a Kind. https://biblia.com/bible/nasb95/Luke%201.34-38

N. A. (2016). Free from sin but living in bondage? The gossip 4 Jesus initiative. https://gossipforjesus.com/2016/01/21free-from-sin-but-living-in-bondage/

Noyes, P. (2022). 10 roles of the Holy Spirit in the life of Christians. https://www.christianity.com/author/penny-noyes/

Oxford English Dictionary. (2003). Oxford University Press. United Kingdom.

Rohr, R. (2011). Breathing Under Water; Spirituality and the Twelve Steps. Franciscan Media.

The Holy Bible English Standard Version (ESV). (2008) Crossway Books.

The Holy Bible- King James Version, (KJV) Holman Bible publishers, Nashville Tennessee

The Holy Bible, The New American Standard Bible. (NASB)(2019) Lockman Foundation, La Habra, California.

Webster, M. (2022) The Merriam-Webster Dictionary, New Edition. https:// www.amazon.com, Mass-Market Paperback.

Westside Church, The Greater Works Church, 31 days of prayer and fasting (2018). Lewisville, Texas 75067.

Printed in the United States
by Baker & Taylor Publisher Services